F. M. BLACK MIDDLE SCHOOL
1575 Chantilly
Houston, TX 77018

World Soccer Stars ⚽ Estrellas del fútbol mundial™

Didier Drogba

José María Obregón

English translation: Megan Benson

PowerKiDS press.

Editorial Buenas Letras™

New York

Published in 2009 by The Rosen Publishing Group, Inc.
29 East 21st Street, New York, NY 10010

First Edition

Editor: Nicole Pristash
Book Design: Nelson Sa
Layout Design: Julio Gil

Photo Credits: Cover (left, right), pp. 5, 9, 13, 15 © Getty Images; pp. 7, 11, 17, 19, 21 © AFP/Getty Images.

Library of Congress Cataloging-in-Publication Data

Obregón, José María, 1963–
    Didier Drogba / José María Obregón. — 1st ed.
        p. cm. — (World soccer stars = Estrellas del fútbol mundial)
    Includes index.
    English and Spanish.
    ISBN 978-1-4358-2967-1 (library binding)
    1. Drogba, Didier, 1978– 2. Soccer players—Côte d'Ivoire—Biography. I. Title.
    GV942.7.D76O27 2009
    796.334092—dc22
    [B]
                                        2008033078

Manufactured in the United States of America

Contents

Contenido

Didier Drogba is one of the best soccer players in the world. Drogba was born on March 11, 1978, in the city of Abidjan, in Ivory Coast.

Didier Drogba es uno de los mejores futbolistas del mundo. Drogba nació el 11 de marzo de 1978, en la ciudad de Abiyán, en Costa de Marfil.

When Drogba was young, he dreamed of becoming a great soccer player. Today, Drogba is one of the best-known players from Africa.

Cuando Drogba era pequeño soñaba con convertirse en un gran jugador de fútbol. Hoy, es uno de los deportistas más populares de África.

In 2003, Drogba became a member of the team Olympique de Marseille, in France. In his first year with Olympique, he scored 19 **goals**. He was also named the best soccer player in France.

En 2003, Drogba se unió al Olympique de Marsella, en Francia. En su primer año con el Olympique, Drogba **anotó** 19 goles y fue nombrado jugador del año en Francia.

Drogba plays the striker position, so he scores goals. He is very strong and fast. Drogba has scored more than 150 goals!

Drogba juega como delantero. Drogba anota goles. Drogba es muy rápido y muy fuerte. ¡Drogba ha anotado más de 150 goles en su carrera!

When Drogba was 26, he became a member of the team Chelsea, in England. Drogba helped Chelsea win the English Premier League **tournament** in 2005 and 2006.

A los 26 años, Drogba se unió al equipo Chelsea de Inglaterra. Drogba ayudó al Chelsea a ganar el **torneo** de la Liga Premier de Inglaterra en 2005 y en 2006.

Drogba also plays for Ivory Coast's soccer team. Drogba helped the team get to its first **World Cup** in Germany in 2006. Drogba scored Ivory Coast's first World Cup goal.

Drogba también juega en la selección de Costa de Marfil. Drogba ayudó a que su país participara en su primera **Copa del Mundo**, en Alemania 2006. Drogba anotó el primer gol de la historia de su país.

Didier Drogba was named the best player from Ivory Coast in 2007. That same year, Drogba was also named the Best African Player. This was one of Drogba's most important honors.

Didier Drogba fue nombrado el mejor jugador de Costa de Marfil en 2007. Ese mismo año, Drogba recibió el premio como Mejor Jugador Africano de Fútbol. Este es uno de los mayores reconocimientos.

In April 2008, Drogba scored two goals for Chelsea in a European **Champions** League game. Drogba helped Chelsea reach the final, or last, game in the tournament.

En abril de 2008, Drogba anotó dos goles en la semifinal de la **Copa de Campeones** de Europa. Drogba ayudó al Chelsea a jugar su primera final en este importante torneo.

Didier Drogba is a goodwill ambassador for the **United Nations** Development Programme. As an ambassador, Drogba helps make life better in many African countries.

Didier Drogba es embajador de buena voluntad del Programa de las **Naciones Unidas** para el Desarrollo. Así, Drogba ayuda a mejorar la vida de muchos países de África.

Glossary / Glosario

champions (**cham**-pee-unz) The best, or the winners.

goals (**gohlz**) Times when someone puts the ball in the net to score points.

tournament (**tor**-nuh-ment) A group of games to decide the best team.

United Nations (yoo-**ny**-ted **nay**-shunz) A group formed to keep peace between countries.

World Cup (**wur**-uld **kup**) A soccer tournament that takes place every four years with the best teams from around the world.

---

anotar Conseguir uno o varios goles.

Copa de Campeones (la) Competición de fútbol en la que juegan los mejores clubes de Europa.

Copa del Mundo (la) Competición de fútbol, cada 4 años, en la que juegan los mejores equipos del mundo.

Naciones Unidas (las) Organización que se encarga de mantener la paz entre los países.

torneo (el) Grupo de partidos que se juegan para encontrar al mejor equipo.

Resources / Recursos

Books in English/Libros en inglés

Shea, Therese. *Soccer Stars*. Danbury, CT:
Children's Press, 2007.

Bilingual Books/Libros bilingües

Contró, Arturo. *Rafael Márquez*. New York: Rosen
Publishing/Buenas Letras, 2008.

Web Sites

Due to the changing nature of Internet links,
Rosen Publishing has developed an online list of
Web sites related to the subject of this book. This
site is updated regularly. Please use this link to
access the list:

www.buenasletraslinks.com/ss/drogba/

Index

Índice

DATE DUE

HIGHSMITH 45230